animals**animals**

Zebras

by **Katherine Noble-Goodman**

Marshall Cavendish
Benchmark
New York

Series consultant:
James G. Doherty
General Curator, Bronx Zoo, New York

Marshall Cavendish Benchmark
99 White Plains Road
Tarrytown, NY 10591-9001
www.marshallcavendish.us

Library of Congress Cataloging-in-Publication Data

Noble-Goodman, Katherine.
Zebras / by Katherine Noble-Goodman.— 1st ed.
p. cm. — (Animals, animals)
Summary: "Describes the physical characteristics, behavior, and habitat of zebras"—Provided by publisher.
Includes bibliographical references and index.
ISBN 0-7614-1871-7
1. Zebras—Juvenile literature. I. Title. II. Series.

QL737.U62N64 2004
599.665'7—dc22
2004021463

Photo research by Joan Meisel

Cover photo: Heinrich Van Den Berg/WWI/Peter Arnold, Inc.

The photographs in this book are used by permission and through the courtesy of:
Animals Animals: Joe McDonald, 26; Manoj Shah, 32; Austin Stevens, 34. *Bruce Coleman, Inc.:* K&K Ammann, 17.
Corbis: Paul A. Souders, 4; Joe McDonald, 10; Martin Harvey, 11; Stapleton Collection, 16; Michael S. Lewis, 39.
Peter Arnold, Inc.: C. & M. Denis-Huot, 1, 24, 27, 28, 33; Michael J. Minardi, 6; Martin Harvey, 9; Gerard Lacz, 22;
Heinrich Van Den Berg/WWI, 30, 40; Frans Lemmens, 36. *Photo Researchers, Inc.:* Andrew Rakoczy, 7; Tim Davis, 14;
Christophe Ratier, 21; Renee Lynn, 38.

Series design by Adam Mietlowski

Printed in China

1 3 5 6 4 2

Contents

1 Introducing Zebras 5

2 Life on the Savanna 15

3 Born on the Plains 25

4 The Challenge of Survival 31

5 An Uncertain Future 37

Glossary 42

Find Out More 46

Index 48

1 Introducing Zebras

What do you see when you look at a zebra's flashy stripes? Do you see white stripes on a black background? Or do you see black stripes on white? You might think the answer is obvious, but it's not. Even scientists disagree as to which answer is right.

There are three *species* of zebras—plains, Grevy's, and mountain—and each has a slightly different pattern of stripes. A fourth type of zebra with brown and white stripes was hunted to *extinction* more than one hundred years ago. It was called a quagga.

No one knows for sure why zebras have stripes. It might be that the stripes help to confuse lions, hyenas, and any of the other animals that hunts zebras.

Some people look at zebras and see white animals with black stripes. Others see black animals with white stripes. What do you see?

Each zebra has a different stripe pattern. When a herd is gathered on the plains, the stripes blend and blur together. This makes it hard for a lion or hyena to single out one to attack.

When a herd of zebras takes off running, the stripes blur together making it hard for a *predator* to single out one zebra to attack. This confusion works especially well at night. But there are other possible reasons why zebras have stripes. White stripes may help keep zebras cool in the hot African sun. Or the stripes possibly attract fewer biting flies than solid colors would.

One thing scientists know for sure about zebras' mysterious coats is that no two are exactly alike. Each one is as unique as a human fingerprint. Zebras can tell one another apart by the pattern of their stripes. That calls for good eyesight.

Zebras have developed unique eyes that aid their survival. Set far apart and high on their faces, zebras can see what is happening on either side of them at the same time. They can even look back and forth without turning their heads or moving their eyes. This is helpful on the African *plains,* where zebras must always be on the lookout for predators.

Large, wide-set eyes help zebras spot dangers on the open plains. Zebras use their eyes to look in opposite directions at the same time.

Species Chart

Adults

(general range for all species)

Height: from the shoulder, 4 to 5 feet (1.2 to 1.5 meters)
Weight: 385 to 990 pounds (175 to 449 kilograms)
Length (body): 6 to 9 feet (1.8 to 2.7 meters)
Length (tail): 17 to 22 inches (44 to 55 centimeters)
Life Span: 15 to 30 years, in the wild

Foals

Height: from the shoulder, at birth, 33 inches (84 centimeters)
Weight: at birth, 55 to 88 pounds (25 to 40 kilograms)

Plains Zebra

The plains zebra is the most common species found in zoos. Their short legs and round bellies give them a stout, almost fat appearance. Their stripes are thin and close together on their front half, and broad and spread apart toward their rump. Stripes continue around the belly. The white stripes often have a brown streak in the middle, creating what looks like a shadow.

Species Chart

Grevy's Zebra

Grevy's zebra is the largest of the three species, weighing up to 990 pounds (450 kilograms). Their stripes are thin and close together. Their bellies and a line around their tails are completely white. Grevy's zebras are easy to tell apart from other species because they have large, round ears like a mule.

Mountain Zebra

Mountain zebras are sleeker and thinner than the other two zebra species. Their hooves are narrower, for climbing in the foothills. They have a dewlap, or a loose fold of skin hanging from their neck. On the main part of their bodies, the white stripes are thin, making the black stripes appear that much wider. This pattern changes as the stripes become thicker and the same width over their rumps. Their bellies are white, while their noses are dark.

Zebras once filled the plains of eastern and southern Africa. Through the years their range, or home territory, has shrunk more and more.

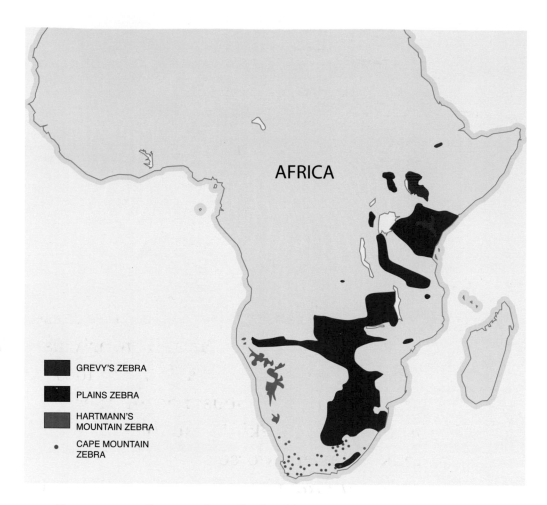

AFRICA

GREVY'S ZEBRA

PLAINS ZEBRA

HARTMANN'S MOUNTAIN ZEBRA

CAPE MOUNTAIN ZEBRA

Scientists have divided all plants and animals into groups called families. Zebras belong to the equid family. The different animal groups that make up a family usually look and act quite similar to one another. Relatives of zebras include horses, donkeys, and mules. All these equids have powerful legs, a long face with large ears, hooves, a mane, and a tail.

12

It probably will not come as a surprise to learn that at one time, humans tried to make zebras do the same work that horses did. Roman gladiators attempted to train zebras to pull their special carts called chariots. Later, when Europeans first settled Africa, they used zebras to pull plows on their farms. But the stubborn, sometimes ornery zebras never liked these jobs. They were not dependable workers like the *domesticated* horse. Eventually, humans decided to leave zebras alone to roam the plains of Africa.

Life in the wild has not been easy for these striped mammals. Today, there are not nearly as many zebras as there were just a few decades ago. Hunters have killed thousands of these animals for their tough skins and beautiful coats. To make matters worse, much of the zebras' natural *habitat* is now farmland for crops and cattle.

Did You Know . . .

You can tell species of zebras apart by their stripes. The Grevy's stripes are thin and close together. Mountain zebras have narrow stripes on their torsos and wider stripes on their rumps. The plains zebras' stripes are wide, and they often have lighter "shadow" stripes between their bold black and white stripes. Their stripes meet under their bellies and extend down their legs.

2 Life on the Savanna

It is almost the end of the dry season on the African *savanna*, and a herd of more than a hundred zebras is enjoying an afternoon of grazing, grooming, and playing. They have stopped to eat the last bits of grass left on the plains before they begin their 300-mile (483-kilometer) journey to their rainy season home on the *Serengeti*. There are several families or *harems* of zebras in the herd. A harem is a group of ten to sixteen zebras that includes one adult male, or stallion, several adult females, or mares, and foals that are not yet old enough to leave their mothers and join another harem.

Zebras tend to stay in groups, either as part of herds or harems. Joining forces and sticking together offer the zebras greater protection and safety.

The Quagga

The quagga is a *subspecies* of the plains zebra that was hunted to extinction by the end of the 1800s. It had fewer stripes than the plains zebra, and its stripes were light brown instead of black. Its tail was white. A group called the Quagga Breeding Project is trying to do something no one has ever done before—breed an animal back from extinction. The group's members pick plains zebras that look most like quaggas and then breed them. The scientists are hoping that over time, the offspring of these plains zebras will look more and more like the quagga. Eventually, they hope a baby will be born that looks exactly like this extinct subspecies.

These zebras are actually playing, practicing for the day they will fight older stallions to earn the right to set up harems of their own.

Under the shade of an acacia tree, the zebras that make up one of the herd's many harems turn their attention to grooming. Standing tail to nose and nose to tail in this uniquely zebra pose, they nibble and scratch insects and dirt off each others' backs. When they grow tired of grooming, they rest their chins in the same spot on the back of their partner. When zebras stand like this, they can see in all directions, watching the savanna for signs of danger.

Nearby, a group of young males pretends to fight. They snort and stomp in playful anger, nipping at each others' necks and kicking up dust with their back legs.

The Zebra:

Related to the horse, the zebra is a graceful animal . . .

Inside and Out

. . . and a swift runner when it has to be.

They are practicing for the time when they will be old enough to challenge a *dominant* stallion for a chance to claim a female and to start harems of their own. Males are usually not ready to do this until they are about three or four years old. So, for now, the fighting is just a game.

Part of the herd has found a smooth spot on the ground for a dust bath. They line up and take turns flopping onto their backs, kicking their heels in the air and twisting their shoulders and hips. This is how zebras scratch and clean their skin. A young mare has just finished her bath. She rolls onto her side and springs back onto her feet. She twitches and shakes herself off, *nickering* and snorting the whole time.

Zebras communicate using a range of sounds including *whinnies* and squeals. They also use body language to express themselves. A stallion may fold his ears back and swish his tail when he does not wish to be disturbed. Trotting up to his favorite mare, tossing his head up and down, and then nuzzling her neck all serve as signs of affection.

Back on the savanna, the grooming and playing suddenly stop. The zebras lift their heads and prick their ears forward to listen. Then, as if on cue, they all

Whether in the dirt or on the grass, a dust bath helps zebras scratch those hard-to-reach places.

To communicate zebras make use of many different sounds. This zebra seems to be sending an urgent message, perhaps to a foal that has wandered too far.

turn and walk in the same direction, falling into a single-file line behind the herd's dominant female. The dominant stallion brings up the rear, and the zebras begin their *migration*, heading south across Kenya and into Tanzania. A herd of migrating zebras always lines up in the same order. Scientists believe that each zebra knows its place in line by memorizing the stripe pattern of the zebra it follows.

3 Born on the Plains

The rains have arrived on the Serengeti, and the dry, barren plains quickly turn green with new grass. It is time for the pregnant females to give birth. Mares lie down to have their babies, with their stallion posted nearby watching for predators. If the male spots approaching danger, he lets out a loud squeal of alarm. Amazingly, the mare can stop her labor and wait for a safer time to have her baby.

After the baby is born, the mother shields her new foal from the other zebras, even the new baby's older brothers and sisters. During the first few hours and days of a baby zebra's life, it must memorize the pattern of its mother's stripes. This process is called *imprinting*.

To remove any lingering scent that might attract a predator, a mother licks her baby's fur right after giving birth.

This zebra is only a few weeks old and is already learning how to survive on the plains. By the time foals are four months old, they seek out other baby zebras for play—always within sight of their watchful mothers.

If it sees another zebra during this time, it may become confused and think the other zebra is actually its mother. This would have tragic results for the foal because, unlike many other animals, female zebras will not take care of another mother's *offspring*.

Alone with her new foal, the mother licks her baby's wet fur. Its chocolate brown and white coat is fuzzy and soft. The baby struggles to stand, but its long, wobbly legs are still weak. At first it stumbles and falls, but within an hour, it is up nursing on its mother's warm, rich milk. The baby survives on milk alone for the first few weeks. Then it begins to graze.

Zebras start eating grass when they are just a few weeks old. But they rely on their mothers' milk for most of their meals for at least eight months— sometimes longer.

Zebras fight by biting as well as rearing up and kicking with their long legs. This may be a serious fight, but it could also be a form of play.

Foals stay with their mothers for two to three years. Then, the young males join a *bachelor* herd, where they live until they are three to six years old and are strong enough to start their own harems. In order to do that, a stallion needs a mare. To claim one, the stallion may have to prove himself in a fight. This is when all the fighting practice proves useful. First, the young stallion tries to steal a mare from a harem. One of the herd's older or dominant stallions notices, however, and moves in to stop his daughter from leaving. If the young stallion does not run off, the pair will fight—kicking, biting, and chasing each other—sometimes for several hours. The older stallion is testing the younger male to see if he is strong and brave enough to be a good match for his daughter. Rarely does a young male win one of his first fights with an older, more experienced stallion. When the younger stallion does hold his ground, the father lets his daughter go and a new zebra family is formed.

4 The Challenge of Survival

Zebra are *herbivores* that eat mainly grass. Some zebras also eat leaves and shoots, and if they cannot find anything else to eat, they will dig up roots with their hooves. They never stray far from water. Unlike some African animals that can go for a long time without drinking, most zebras must drink water every day.

Because they have strong front teeth, zebras can tear off the tops of grasses that are too tough for other animals. Wildebeests and gazelles often graze alongside zebras, eating the shorter grass these "lawnmowers of the Serengeti" have left behind. Zebras have to eat a lot to get full. They spend up to eighteen hours per day just eating. Zebras do so much grinding with their strong

Plains and Grevy's zebras need water almost every day to survive. Mountain zebras can go three or four days without taking a drink.

jaw muscles that the molars in the back of their mouths continue to grow their entire lives. If the teeth did not keep growing, zebras would grind them down to nothing in just a few years.

Zebras rely on the grass of the savanna for most of their food. With their strong teeth and jaws, they are able to eat grass that is too tough for most other grazers.

Zebras also spend much of their time trying to avoid being eaten by one of their many predators. Hyenas and leopards hunt zebras, and zebras are lions' main source of food. A full-grown zebra can often outrun its predator, but during birthing season when there are many young foals in the herd, running from predators is not always possible. Often, the predator goes after the foal. When this happens, the foal's mother and father, and sometimes other members of the herd or harem, will try and protect it by kicking and stomping at the predator.

An animal living on the savanna must constantly be on the lookout for predators. Zebras will not go back to grazing until they are sure all danger has passed.

33

Typically, lions prey on the slow and weak members of a zebra herd.
This male lion is feasting on an adult zebra that may have been hunted
down by a group of lionesses.

Once, a stallion was even seen picking up a hyena in his teeth and slamming it to the ground. Adult zebras also defend one another, but once a zebra—young or old—becomes the target of a hungry *carnivore*, it often loses the battle.

Even at night, zebras are on the lookout for danger. They have excellent nighttime vision. Stallions take turns keeping watch. All adult zebras sleep standing up, so they are ready to run or defend themselves in an instant. Only very young zebras regularly lie down to sleep.

Did You Know . . .

Zebras' hooves are made of keratin, a strong but flexible material that lets them run over the hard, uneven savanna. It also allows them to cross rocky terrain without getting sore feet. Zebras can reach speeds of up to 40 miles (64 kilometers) per hour.

5 An Uncertain Future

Life on the African savanna is never easy, especially for herbivores like zebras. They are always at risk of becoming another animal's next meal. On its own, nature is able to keep the various animal populations in balance, and until recently, the savanna was full of these graceful relatives of the horse. But today, zebras face a new threat—the growing human population.

Humans have taken much of the land in Africa that was home to wild animals and turned it into farms and villages. Grasslands where zebras once roamed freely are now fenced off as pastures for cows or as fields for crops. Rivers in some areas are drained nearly dry to water crops. This habitat loss is the main reason zebras and other animals are becoming *endangered* or extinct.

Humans and zebras have shared life on the African plains for thousands of years.

37

Like most places in the world, Africa's human population is growing rapidly. More and more natural habitat is claimed each year for communities and farmland.

Today, both the mountain zebra and Grevy's zebra are endangered, and the population of plains zebras is shrinking. Grevy's zebras are especially in trouble. In the late 1970s, there were about 15,000 Grevy's living in Africa. Today, there are only 3,000 to 3,500. More than half a million plains zebra survive in Africa, but even this species, which once roamed the plains by the millions, is losing its habitat. Without protection, it may become endangered, too.

In order to grow, crops—such as the tea leaves this farmer is picking—
need more than land. They also need water, which is often taken from
lakes, streams, and watering holes where animals go to drink.

Zebras are social animals. These two greet each other with a friendly nuzzle.

What can be done to save the zebras?

Like all wild animals, the best way to protect zebras is to protect their habitat. One way to do this is to set aside wildlife areas and to pass laws that make it illegal for humans to change the land or disturb the animals. Governments in Africa have set up many national parks and game preserves where hunting, farming, and development are not allowed. One such place is the Mountain Zebra National Park in South Africa. The park was created in 1937 to save one subspecies of mountain zebra, the cape zebra, from extinction. At that time, there were only six left. By 1964 the population had grown to twenty-five, and today, there are more than two hundred cape mountain zebras in the national park. With more success stories like this one, these mysteriously striped creatures will continue to roam the vast African plains for years to come.

Did You Know...
Zebras live throughout the southern and eastern parts of Africa. Most zebras live on the grasslands and savannas. Mountain zebras live in hilly areas and on steeper slopes.

Glossary

bachelor: A young male zebra not yet old enough to mate with females.

carnivore: An animal that eats other animals.

domesticated: Taken from the wild by humans and tamed, trained, and bred.

dominant: Usually the strongest and sometimes the oldest animal in the herd. In zebra herds, there is a dominant male and a dominant female.

endangered: At a high risk of becoming extinct in the wild.

extinct: No longer surviving in the wild or anywhere else.

habitat: The natural surroundings or environment where an animal lives.

harem: A group of zebras that includes one mature stallion, several mares, and foals that are not yet old enough to leave their mothers and form harems of their own.

herbivore: An animal that feeds only on plants such as grasses, shrubs, and other vegetation.

imprinting: The process by which a newborn animal forms an attachment to the first object or animal it sees, usually its mother.

migration: The seasonal movement of animals from one place to another, usually in search of new feeding grounds.

nicker: To neigh or make a sound like a horse.

offspring: The descendants of a person, animal, or plant; the next generation.

plains: A large, flat, often treeless area of land, usually covered with grass and bushes.

predator: An animal that hunts and kills other animals for food.

prey: An animal hunted or caught for food.

savanna: A type of grassland with widely spaced trees and grass.

Serengeti: A region in Tanzania about the size of the state of Connecticut. Its name comes from the Maasai word *Siringit,* meaning "endless plains." More than a million mammals and birds live there.

species: A group of animals that has the same physical traits and can mate and produce similar offspring.

subspecies: An animal that is much like the species it belongs to but that lives in a different area and looks different in a specific way.

whinny: To neigh, especially in a low and gentle manner.

Find Out More

Books

Cole, Melissa. *Zebras.* Farmington Hills, MI: Blackbirch Press, 2002.

Grimbly, Shona. *Endangered! Zebras.* New York: Benchmark Books, 1999.

Holmes, Kevin J. *Zebras.* Mankato, MN: Bridgestone Books, 2000.

MacDonald, David. *The Encyclopedia of Mammals.* Oxford, England: Equinox, 1995.

Stuart, Chris, and Tilde Stuart. *Africa's Vanishing Wildlife.* Washington, D.C.: Smithsonian Books, 1996.

Wexo, John B. *Zebras.* San Diego: Wildlife Education, 1999.

Videos

Zebras: Patterns in the Grass. National Geographic Society, 1999.

Web Sites

African Wildlife Foundation Zebra
http://www.awf.org/wildlives/151

San Diego Zoo Animal Bytes Zebra Page
http://www.sandiegozoo.org/animalbytes/t-zebra.html

International Museum of Horses Zebra Page
http://www.imh.org/imh/bw/zebra.html

Animal Diversity Web Zebra Page
http://animaldiversity.ummz.umich.edu/site/accounts/classification/Equus.html

Index

Page numbers for illustrations are in **boldface**.

map, 12

dewlap, 11
dust bath, 20, **21**

ears, 10, 12, 20,
equids, 12
extinction, 5, 16, 37
eyesight, 6–7, **7**, 35

fighting, 17, **17**, 20, **28**, 29
foals, 15, **24**, 25, **26**, 27, **27**, 29, 33
food, 15, 27, 31, 32, **32**

grooming, 17, 20

habitat, 13, 37, 38, 41
harems, 13, 17, 20, 29, 33
herbivores, 31, 37
herd, 6, **14**, 15, 17, 20, 23, 29, 33

hooves, 12, 35
horses, 12, 13, 18, 37
hyenas, 5, 33, 35

imprinting, 25

legs, 9, 12, 13, 27, **28**
lions, 5, 33, **34**

mares, 15, 20, 25, 29
migration, 15, 23
Mountain Zebra National Park, 41
mules, 10, 12

plains, 7, 13, 25, 37, 41
predators, 5, 6, 7, 25, 33

quagga, 5, 16, **16**

savanna, 15, 20, 37, 41
Serengeti, 15, 25, 31

skeleton, **18**
species chart, 8–11
stallions, 15, 20, 23, 25, 29, 35
stripes, **4**, 5, 6, **6**, 9, 10, 11, 13, 16

teeth, 31, 32, 35

zebras,
    Grevy's, 5, 10, **10**, 13, 38
    and humans, 13, 37–41, **37**
    mountain, 5, 11, **11**, 13, 38, 41
    plains, 5, 9, **9**, 13, 16, 38

About the Author

Katherine Noble-Goodman writes and teaches about environment. She is also the author of numerous articles and other publications, including the *Oregon Wildlife Foundation's Guide to Endangered Animals*. This is her first children's book.

The North Pole Mystery

WRITTEN BY MARY BLOUNT CHRISTIAN
ILLUSTRATED BY JOE BODDY

Milliken Publishing Company, St. Louis, Missouri

© 1989 by Milliken Publishing Company

Cover Design by Henning Design, St. Louis, Missouri

Library of Congress Catalog Card Number: 88-60633
ISBN 0-88335-597-3 (pbk.)/ISBN 0-88335-593-0 (lib. bdg.)

David Cooper was sitting on his front steps.
His friends Ann and Walter came up.
"What are you doing?" Ann asked him.

"I'm reading my new book," David said.
"And I'm watching Adam for Mother."

"That's funny," Walter said.
"I see your book, but I don't see Adam."

David laid down his book.
"He was here a minute ago.
Adam!" he called. "Where are you?"
There was no answer.

"Maybe he went into the house," Ann said.

1

David went inside.
He looked in each room.
Adam was not in the house.

Next, David ran outside.
"Adam!" David called.

Pedro came over. "What's up?" he asked.

"Adam is gone," David said. "He is a pest.
But I love my little brother. I'm afraid.
Where can he be? I'll look in the backyard."

"I'll look down Sherlock Street," Walter said.

"I'll look up Sherlock Street," Ann said.

"And I'll look across Sherlock Street," Pedro said.

The four children ran off.
"Adam!" they called.
There was no answer.

3

Later the children went
back to David's house.
"I have an idea," Walter said.
"I'll call my dog, Watson.
Watson can find Adam."

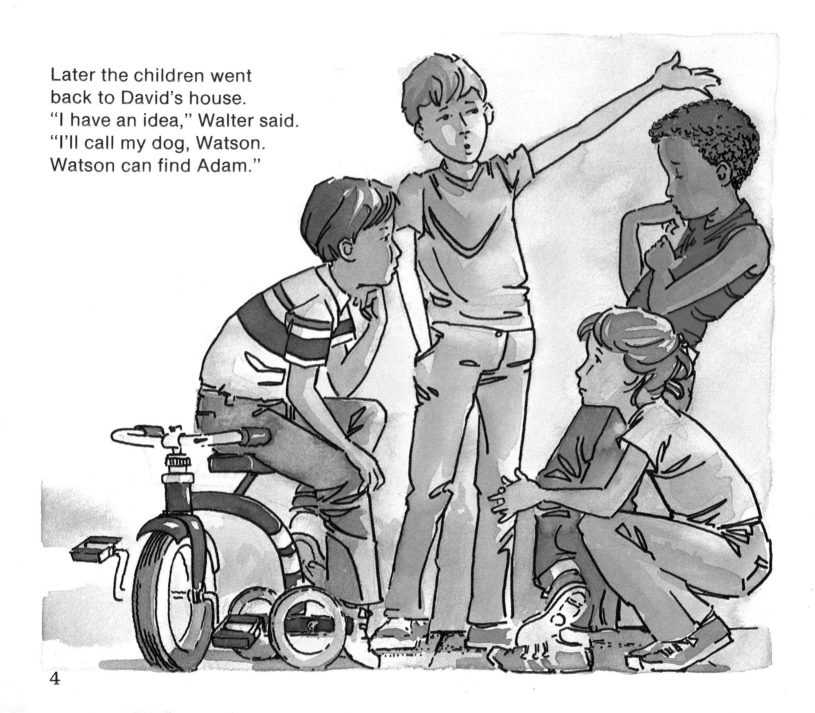

Ann laughed. "Watson cannot find his own tail!"

Walter's face turned red. "Just you wait!
You will see! Watson will help us find Adam."

Pedro looked up. "The sun is behind the trees,"
he said. "It will be dark in a few hours."

"Get Watson, Walter," David said.
"Maybe he can help us find Adam."

5

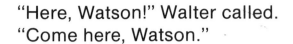

"Here, Watson!" Walter called.
"Come here, Watson."

Watson ran to Walter.
"Woof! Woof!" he said.

"Good dog, Watson," Walter said.
"Go find Adam." Watson sat down.

"No, Watson," Walter said.
"Adam. Find Adam."
Watson rolled over.

"Your dog cannot find Adam,"
David said. "What can we do?
I should have watched Adam.
I should have played with him,
but I read my book instead."
David put his head in his hands.
Ann put her hand on his shoulder.

"Don't worry, David," she said.
"We will find him."

Walter kept a notebook in his pocket.
He pulled it out. He pulled out his pencil too.
"When did you last see Adam?" Walter asked.

"What a good idea!" Pedro said.
"Walter can write all the clues
in his notebook."

"When we have all the clues,
we will find Adam," Ann said.

Watson stood on his back legs.
"Woof! Woof!" he said.

"Stop that, Watson," Walter said.
"We have to think about clues.
First, when did Adam leave?"

"I don't know," David said.

"What did Adam have on?" Walter asked.

"That does not matter," Ann said.
"We know he is gone.
And we know what he looks like.
What we need to know is what
you were doing before he left."

10

"Adam wanted to go for a walk,"
David said. "I didn't want to go.
I tried to make him think about something else.
I showed him my compass.
I told him it was like magic.
I showed him how the needle
always points toward the North Pole.
Adam said the compass pointed to Santa's house.
He loves to hear about Santa."

David looked around. "My compass is gone!
Adam must have it."

Walter wrote in his notebook:

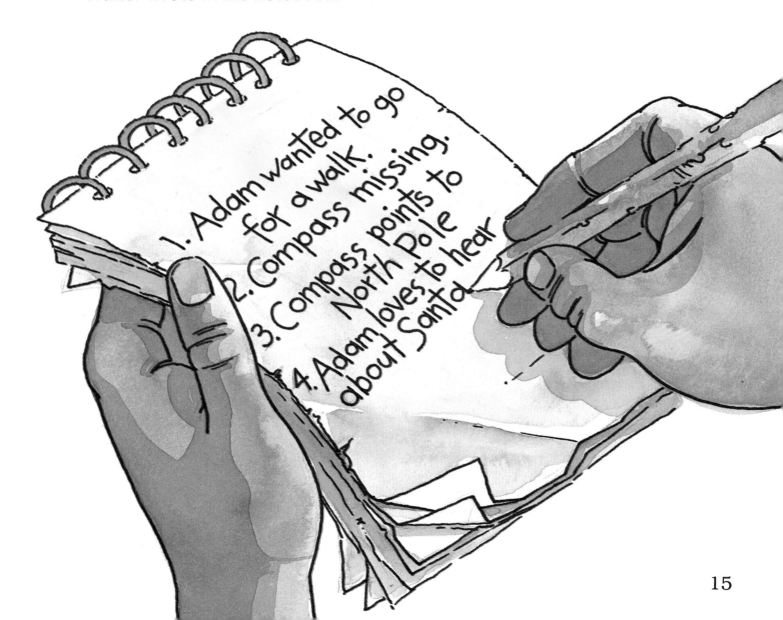

1. Adam wanted to go for a walk.
2. Compass missing.
3. Compass points to North Pole
4. Adam loves to hear about Santa

"I think Adam has gone for a walk," Walter said.
"And I think he needed your compass to get
where he wanted to go."

Ann clapped her hands.
"Adam is walking to the North Pole!
He is following the compass needle!"

16

"Then we must follow a compass needle too," Pedro said.
"Does anyone have a compass?"

Everyone said no.

"Then we will have to make one," Pedro said.
"We need a magnet with the ends marked *N* and *S*,
a thin piece of cork, a plastic bowl,
a needle, and some glue."

The children got the things they needed.
Pedro filled the bowl with water.

18

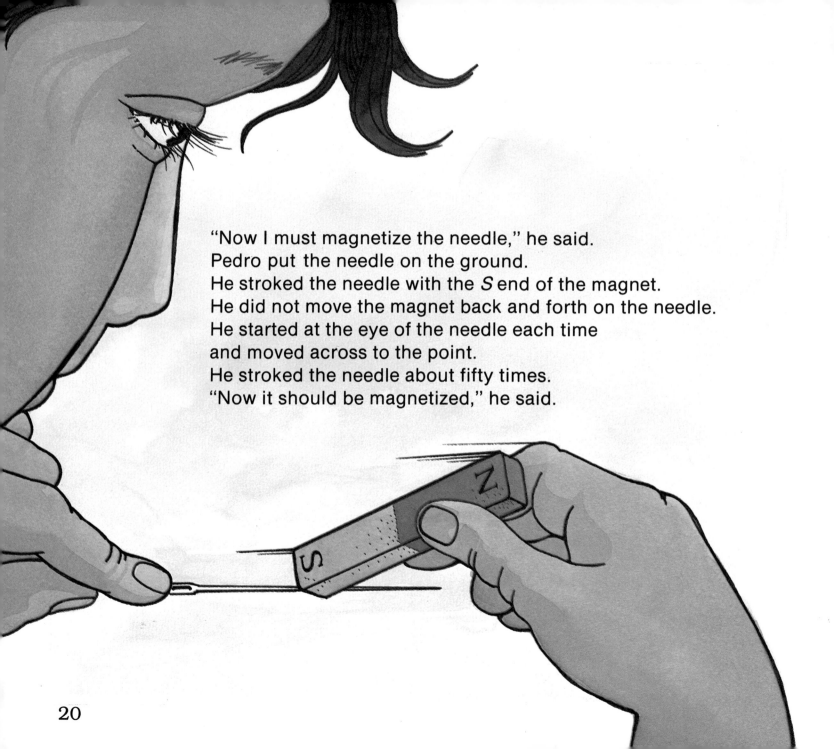

"Now I must magnetize the needle," he said.
Pedro put the needle on the ground.
He stroked the needle with the *S* end of the magnet.
He did not move the magnet back and forth on the needle.
He started at the eye of the needle each time
and moved across to the point.
He stroked the needle about fifty times.
"Now it should be magnetized," he said.

Pedro glued the needle onto the cork.
Then he put the cork into the water.
The needle turned in the water and then stopped.
"The sharp end of this magnetized needle
is pointing to the north,"
Pedro told his friends.

22

The children walked to
where the needle pointed.
They went down David's driveway.
They went past the garage.
They went past the tree house.
They went right to the back fence!

"Adam cannot get over this fence," David said.
"It is too tall."

"Woof! Woof!" Watson said.

Ann laughed and pointed.
"Look at that silly dog!
Now he is barking at a tree!"

Watson stood on his back legs.
He put his front paws on the tree.
"Woof! Woof!" he said.

"He is not barking at the tree," Walter said.
"He is barking at something *in* the tree.
And I think I know what it is!"

Walter went up the tree.
Ann, David, and Pedro went up too.

There in the tree house they found Adam sound asleep.
He still had David's compass in his hand.

"Adam, wake up!" David said.
He put his arms around Adam.
"I'm so glad you are all right."

"I was going to the North Pole without you," Adam said.

"This isn't the North Pole," David said.

"I know," Adam said.
"But I couldn't really go there.
Mother won't let me cross the street by myself."

David laughed. "I'm glad.
Let's go into the house.
It's time to eat."

"Thank you for your help," David told his friends.

"Woof! Woof!" Watson said.

"Thank you too, Watson," David said.

Walter put his notebook away.
"We are very good detectives," he said.
"We should call ourselves the
Sherlock Street Detectives."

"Yes!" the others said.

"Woof! Woof!"

"Yes, you too, Watson," Walter said.

Watson rolled over on his back.

"Woof! Woof!"

Glossary

compass – Something used to show which way north, south, east, and west are. The needle on a compass points to the north.

cork – The outer part of some oak trees. Pieces of cork are pushed into the tops of some bottles to close them.

eye – The hole in a sewing needle.

magnet – A piece of rock or metal that pulls iron or steel toward it.

magnetize – To make something act like a magnet.

needle – The pointer on a compass.

North Pole – The place on earth that is the farthest north.

Vocabulary

across	cross	front	magnetized	plastic	stood
Adam	dark	garage	marked	pocket	street
afraid	David Cooper	glue	matter	point(s)	stroked
Ann	detectives	glued	minute	pointed	tail
answer	driveway	gone	move	pointing	thank
anyone	else	ground	moved	pulled	thin
arms	everyone	head	needle	really	things
around	eye	hear	next	right	toward
backyard	face	hours	north	rolled	tried
barking	fence	idea	North Pole	Santa	turned
behind	few	instead	notebook	sharp	wake
bowl	fifty	kept	others	Sherlock	Walter
brother	filled	know	ourselves	shoulder	watched
children	first	laid	paws	silly	watching
clapped	follow	laughed	Pedro	something	water
clues	following	leave	pencil	sound	Watson
compass	forth	magic	pest	started	won't
cork	found	magnet	piece	steps	worry
couldn't	friends	magnetize			